SandCastle™

Math Made Fun

3-D Shapes Are Like Green Grapes!

Tracy Kompelien

Consulting Editors, Diane Craig, M.A./Reading Specialist
and Susan Kosel, M.A. Education

ABDO
Publishing Company

Published by ABDO Publishing Company, 4940 Viking Drive, Edina, Minnesota 55435.

Printed in the United States.

Credits
Edited by: Pam Price
Curriculum Coordinator: Nancy Tuminelly
Cover and Interior Design and Production: Mighty Media
Photo Credits: AbleStock, ShutterStock, Wewerka Photography

Library of Congress Cataloging-in-Publication Data

Kompelien, Tracy, 1975-
    3-D shapes are like green grapes! / Tracy Kompelien
      p. cm. -- (Math made fun)
    ISBN 10 1-59928-509-6 (hardcover)
    ISBN 10 1-59928-510-X (paperback)

    ISBN 13 978-1-59928-509-2 (hardcover)
    ISBN 13 978-1-59928-510-8 (paperback)
    1. Geometry, Solid--Juvenile literature. 2. Shapes--Juvenile literature. I. Title. II. Series.

QA457.K66 2007
516.23--dc22

                                                                                2006015288

SandCastle Level: Fluent

SandCastle™ books are created by a professional team of educators, reading specialists, and content developers around five essential components—phonemic awareness, phonics, vocabulary, text comprehension, and fluency—to assist young readers as they develop reading skills and strategies and increase their general knowledge. All books are written, reviewed, and leveled for guided reading, early reading intervention, and Accelerated Reader® programs for use in shared, guided, and independent reading and writing activities to support a balanced approach to literacy instruction. The SandCastle™ series has four levels that correspond to early literacy development. The levels help teachers and parents select appropriate books for young readers.

| **Emerging Readers** | **Beginning Readers** | **Transitional Readers** | **Fluent Readers** |
| (no flags) | (1 flag) | (2 flags) | (3 flags) |

These levels are meant only as a guide. All levels are subject to change.

3-D shapes

are shapes that have length, width, and height and take up space.

Words used to describe 3-D shapes:

cone
cube
cylinder
pyramid
rectangular prism
sphere

A  is a sphere.

A sphere is a solid figure

that is perfectly round.

This  is a cone.

A cone is a solid figure

that slopes from a single

point to a circular base.

are cubes.

A cube is a solid figure

with six square faces that

are all the same size.

This is a rectangular prism. A rectangular prism is a solid figure that has six faces. The opposite faces are equal.

This is a cylinder.
A cylinder is a solid figure with two circular faces that are the same distance apart and joined by a curved surface.

This 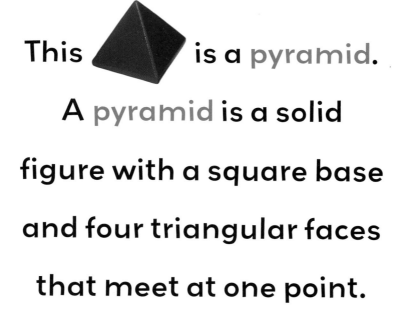 is a pyramid.

A pyramid is a solid figure with a square base and four triangular faces that meet at one point.

3-D Shapes Are Like Green Grapes!

Seth goes ape over any 3-D shape. He sees a sphere in each grape!

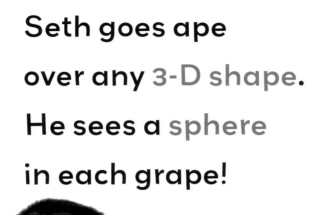

I know that this is a sphere because it is perfectly round.

This is a cylinder because it has a circle at each end.

Since the day he was born, Seth has liked canned corn. He comes running when he hears the scrape of his mom opening a cylindrical shape.

fourteen

14

Seth thinks it's cool to take his lunch to school. As he grabs his lunchbox, he says, "This 3-D shape really rocks!"

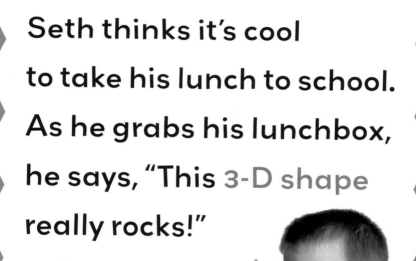

I know that this is a rectangular prism because it has six faces and opposite faces are equal.

3-D Shapes Every Day!

When Sasha studies at school, she uses a globe.

I notice that Earth is round. It is shaped like a sphere.

The books that Sasha sees are in the shape **of** rectangular prisms!

The books each have six faces. Opposite faces are the same size.

twenty
20

Sasha's teacher uses chalk that is in the shape of a cylinder!

This chalk has two circular faces joined by a curved surface.

twenty-two

22

Sometimes at lunch the students get ice-cream cones for dessert! What 3-D shapes do you see when you are at school?

Glossary

equal – having exactly the same size or amount.

face – a side of a 3-D shape. Also called a plane.

length – the distance from one end of an object to the other.

round – having every part of the surface the same distance from the center.

solid figure – a shape that takes up space in three dimensions. Also called a 3-D shape.